ANIMAL FAMILIES

Wolves

General Editor
Tim Harris

WAYLAND

WAYLAND

This edition published in 2014 by Wayland

Copyright © 2014 Brown Bear Books Ltd.

Wayland
Hachette Children's Books
338 Euston Road
London NW1 3BH

Wayland Australia
Level 17/207 Kent Street
Sydney, NSW 2000

All Rights Reserved.

Brown Bear Books Ltd.
First Floor
9–17 St. Albans Place
London
N1 0NX

Managing Editor: Tim Harris
Designer: Lynne Lennon
Picture Manager: Sophie Mortimer
Art Director: Jeni Child
Production Director: Alastair Gourlay
Editorial Director: Lindsey Lowe
Children's Publisher: Anne O'Daly

ISBN: 978-0-7502-8455-4

Printed in China

10 9 8 7 6 5 4 3 2 1

Wayland is a division of Hachette Children's Books,
an Hachette UK company.
www.hachette.co.uk

Picture Credits
Key: t = top, tl = top left, b = bottom, cl = centre left, cr = centre right
Front cover: Thinkstock: iStockphoto, main; **Shutterstock:** Eric Isselee, tr.
Interior: FLPA: Brandenburg, Jim/Minden Pictures 12, 24/25, 29t, Tim Fitzharris/Minden Pictures 10; **iStockphoto:** Lisay 28, Mike UK 29cl; **Shutterstock:** Chris Alcock 6, Critterbiz 4, Avon Dueren 18, Jeff Grabert 27, Intraclique LLC 9, Lori Labrecque 1, 13t, 14, M Lorenz 8, Torsten Lorenz 7, Tom Middleton 26, Arnoud Quanjer 22, Jean-Edouard Rozey 5, Menno Schafer 23, Graham Taylor 16, Pyshnyy Maxim Vjacheslavovich 19; **Thinkstock:** Design Pics 13b, iStockphoto 17, 20, 21cr, Photos.com 21tl, Stockbyte 15.

Contents

Introduction

Wolves are fierce and beautiful creatures. With their strong jaws and sharp teeth they are deadly hunters, but wolves can be gentle and playful, too.

◐ **A wolf has a long snout and pricked-up ears.**

Wolves are creatures of the north. Once they were found throughout the northern hemisphere (Earth north of the equator). Since people have hunted them for centuries, they are now much rarer. Wolves from different parts of the world look a little different from one another.

Despite their different looks, wolves are all one species (type): grey wolf, or *Canis lupus*. Wolves are members of the dog family. Jackals, coyotes and foxes are in the same family. So are the domestic dogs we keep as pets. All breeds of tame dogs are descended from wolves.

Pack hunters

Most wolves live together in a group called a pack. The main purpose of the pack is for hunting. A group of wolves hunting together can kill prey animals much larger than a wolf hunting alone. Reindeer and elk may fall victims to a wolf pack, but a wolf on its own must be content with hunting smaller prey. Wolf cubs also stand a better chance of surviving if they are born in a pack because all the members of the pack help rear them.

The red wolf

Red wolves live in the south-eastern United States. Smaller than grey wolves, they get their name from their reddish fur. Red wolves were once quite common, but now there are only a few hundred left. They were once thought to be crossbreeds between coyotes and grey wolves, but many scientists now believe they are a separate species of wolf.

Captive-breeding programmes have helped increase the population of red wolves.

Living in packs

Most packs contain between five and eight wolves. Small packs may have just two members. A very large pack can have 30 wolves.

Each wolf pack is led by the strongest, most experienced male and female. These are called the alpha male and female, for the first letter of the Greek alphabet. The alpha male and female are the only wolves in the pack that mate and produce young. The other group members are usually their children – young cubs and older offspring born in previous years.

A small wolf pack may contain just two or three animals.

🔵 **The territory of this wolf pack may be 104 square kilometres (40 square miles) in area.**

Knowing their rank

All wolf packs are organised according to a strict hierarchy (ranking order). Below the alpha pair are the next most senior wolves, called the beta male and female. Below them come the younger and less experienced wolves. From the top wolves of the pack to the most junior, each animal knows its rank.

Not all wolves live in a pack. Single wolves may be young animals that have left the pack they grew up in and are searching for other wolves to form a new pack. Other lone wolves are old or sickly.

Territory marks

Groups of wolves defend their territories against rival wolf packs. They mark the borders of their 'patch' by spraying smelly urine on logs and bushes. Other wolves that pass that way smell the scent and know to keep out of the territory. Each wolf has its own scent, so pack members can identify one another by these marks.

Getting the message across

Wolves have many ways of passing information to each another. They can produce a wide range of noises, including snarls, whines and barks.

Wolves in a pack are mostly friendly and affectionate with one another. When two pack members meet, they whine, wag their tails and lick one another's fur. Scientists who study wolves have learned that they have many different facial expressions. They also hold their bodies in different ways to show their feelings and express their rank in the pack. Senior wolves hold their head and tail high and stand up straight to look as big as they can. They hold their ears pricked forward and bare their teeth.

Challenges

Junior wolves use very different 'body language' and expressions. They cower

↩ **If a wolf howls a warning to another pack, other members of the howling wolf's pack often howl their support.**

with their head held low. They lay back their ears, whine and hide their teeth in a tight-lipped grin. A junior wolf will sometimes try to climb the ranking order by snarling at an older wolf. If the senior wolf snarls back, the young wolf often backs down – by rolling over on its back and whimpering. Such behaviour means that real fights are rare.

Tail positions

Wolves also use their tails to show their feelings. Normally, the tail droops down, but top wolves raise theirs high in the air. An aggressive wolf lifts its tail bolt upright in a gesture that means 'watch out!' Young wolves submit (give way) to their seniors by tucking their tails between their legs.

⬆ **A high-ranking wolf bares its teeth and snarls to show a junior wolf that it is the boss.**

Howling

A wolf's howl is an eerie sound, familiar from scary movies! A wolf sticks its nose in the air to produce this drawn-out wail. Other wolves in the pack join in with different notes. Wolves howl to contact members of their group that have got separated. Their calls carry over a long distance. They also howl to rally the group before hunting and to warn rival wolf packs to keep away.

Finding food

Wolves are carnivores – they mostly eat meat. They prefer to hunt and eat large animals such as moose, red deer and wild boar.

These animals are powerful and armed with sharp hooves and fierce antlers or horns. Wolves can only kill them if they are hunting in a pack. Wolves also hunt smaller creatures, such as beavers, hares and squirrels. They also steal domestic animals and eat carrion (dead animals). A hungry wolf will eat fruit and plants or creep silently into city suburbs to scavenge rubbish.

Wolves have good eyesight, but they mainly hunt by smell and hearing. Their sensitive nose can catch even a very faint trace of scent. Their ears are alert to tiny sounds such as breaking twigs that give away hidden prey.

With its ears pricked up to pick up any sounds, a grey wolf silently stalks its prey.

⊕ **Closing in for the kill: a small pack of wolves gets ready to surround and kill a red deer that has an injured leg.**

Lone wolves

Without a pack to hunt with, lone wolves target smaller prey. Nose to the ground, they follow the scent of game birds, hares, squirrels and mice. When the wolf is close enough, it pounces, catching its victim in its front paws.

A hunting wolf pack gradually slinks closer to a herd of grazing moose or red deer. The wolves approach from upwind so their prey do not sense them. They single out young, weak or injured animals that make easy targets.

Wolf attack!

When the wolves are spotted, the chase is on! The speediest wolves run on ahead to surround their prey. Then they dart forward to separate off young or sick animals. The wolves close in from all sides and attack the creature's rump, neck and snout. Finally, one wolf leaps up and kills the chosen victim by biting its neck. A wolf can eat 9 kilograms (20 lbs) of meat at a time. If there are cubs in the den, the wolves hurry back and feed them meat that they have chewed to soften.

Time to mate

Like most members of the dog family, wolves breed only once a year. Mating takes place in late winter. The young grow inside the mother for 63 days.

↻ Newborn cubs are blind. They first open their eyes when they are two or three weeks old.

Wolves time their mating so that the young will be born in spring, just as the weather is getting warmer. Spring comes later in the north than in the south. In mild southern regions, wolves mate in February so that the cubs will be born in April or May. In the icy north, they mate about a month later. There, the cubs are born as spring arrives in late May or June.

Preparing a den

About six weeks after mating, the pregnant female prepares a den for her cubs. She may take over an old fox's lair or a porcupine

Breeding time

The breeding season is a time of tension in the wolf pack. The alpha male and female bully the others to prevent them from mating. Once the top wolves have mated, they stop being aggressive. Life in the pack returns to normal.

burrow and make it bigger. Or she may use a cave or a clump of long grass. When the cubs are due, the other wolves gather and howl with excitement. They sniff the air to find out when the babies are born.

Female wolves usually give birth to a litter (group) of five or six cubs. Newborn cubs weigh only 450 grams (1 lb) and are blind, deaf and helpless. At first, the babies cannot even stand, but the mother pushes them to her nipples and they begin to suck her milk. Slowly, they gain the strength to lead active lives.

At three weeks, cubs can eat small pieces of meat that have been chewed by their mother.

A mother watches over her two cubs, now old enough to walk and jump.

The cubs grow up

After only two or three weeks the cubs are bigger and stronger. They can now hear, and their eyes are open so they can see.

⬇ **By the age of three weeks, a cub is able to wobble to the entrance of the den to look at the outside world.**

The cubs clamber over one another to reach the warmest places under their mother's body. For the first week or so, she rarely leaves them. At first, the cubs feed only on their mother's milk. The other wolves bring half-chewed meat for her to eat, and at three weeks the cubs begin to eat it, too. Soon afterwards, it is time to leave the safety of the den for the outside world. As the

Helping out

All the wolves in the pack help bring up the cubs. The father and other adults, who may be the youngsters' grown-up brothers and sisters, bring food and guard the pups. At about 10 months, the young start to help on hunting trips.

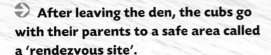 After leaving the den, the cubs go with their parents to a safe area called a 'rendezvous site'.

cubs emerge, the other wolves gather around and wag their tails. They sniff and greet the new members of their pack. When an adult wolf returns from hunting, the cubs are ready. They gather around and lick at the parent's mouth, begging for food. In response the adult wolf arches its body and regurgitates (coughs up) a warm meal of half-digested meat.

Leaving the den

At about eight weeks, the cubs no longer depend on their mother's milk. Then the pups and the parents move to a safe, open area. The pups are left there while the other wolves go hunting. One adult wolf usually stays to 'babysit' the pups. The young begin to learn hunting skills by pouncing on objects such as flowers or feathers. Soon they start catching live prey, such as insects and mice.

Young males

The cubs spend the summer in a safe, grassy spot near their old den. By autumn, they are strong enough to travel with the adults.

Cubs and adults together roam through their territory in search of food. At the age of 10 months, the young wolves are allowed on hunting expeditions. At first, they simply watch what the adults do and learn to keep quiet when the pack is stalking. Later, they act as runners but are not yet old enough to help kill animals.

At one year old the youngsters look like small adult wolves. They reach their full size at the age of 18 months. Most young wolves stay with the pack for two or three years at least. As they grow older, they learn more and more about how to hunt successfully.

⬇ **Young wolves will watch hunts before they are old enough to join in.**

Stay or go?

By the time they are three years old, young males have reached the age when they can breed. Some stay with the same pack all their lives, but many leave at this time. If a young male challenges the leader of his pack and loses, he may be turned out of the group.

⬆ **Young wolves look just like adults by the time they are 18 months old.**

He will wander far and wide, on his own or with his brothers. Eventually, if he survives, he may find a single female or a group of sisters and start a new pack.

Gaining acceptance

Rarely, a young male may be accepted into a different pack. It may take a long time to gain acceptance because the pack members will want to be sure the newcomer is going to be trustworthy.

On the run

The life of a lone male wolf is full of danger. Without a group to hunt with, the young wolf often goes hungry and wanders a long way each day in search of food. Lone wolves are wary and cautious. Wherever possible, they stay out of other wolves' territories. If they are caught trespassing, they may be attacked and killed.

Female wolves

Young females, or she-wolves, can breed when they reach the age of two. During the breeding season, their mothers then see them as a threat.

Alpha females force many of their older daughters out of the pack late in the winter. On their own, young she-wolves face the same dangers as lone males. Like single males, lone she-wolves are wary and watchful. Scent marks on the ground and the noise of wolves howling warn them away from pack territories where they could be attacked.

A she-wolf with one of her cubs. The cub has only recently left its den for the first time.

Ranking among females

Female wolves in the pack follow a strict ranking order, established by fighting. The top female decides where to build her den (right), protects the younger wolves in the pack and may decide when and where the pack goes hunting.

Starting a new pack

The young she-wolf may meet a lone male she can mate with, or she may be allowed to join a band of young wolves. In a new pack, squabbles and fights among the females sort out which animal is the strongest. The most powerful she-wolf becomes the new alpha female. This is the only wolf in the group that will become pregnant, give birth and raise her own cubs.

Shortly before her cubs are born, the alpha male or the other females may help her dig a long underground burrow. As her birth pains begin, the female takes to the den. If she has a large litter of eight cubs or more, it may take up to six hours for all the cubs to be born.

⬇ Life can be very tough for a lone she-wolf, especially when food is scarce in winter.

The body of a hunter

Grey wolves are the largest wild dogs. An adult male wolf may be up to 2.1 metres (7 feet) long from nose to tail-tip and weigh 35 kilograms (75 lbs).

Female wolves are slightly smaller than the males and weigh about 5 kilograms (11 lbs) less. Like most members of the dog family, wolves have five toes on their front feet and four toes on their hind feet. They run on their toes, which means that they take long strides. Their long, strong legs make them tireless runners. Wolves can lope along for many hours if necessary. They can also sprint at up to 45 kilometres per hour (28 mph) for a short distance when they are chasing swift prey.

Jaws and teeth

Wolves have very strong jaws that can bite down with great force. In the front of its mouth are four long, pointed teeth called canines. They are used to seize its prey. At the back of the mouth are large, jagged teeth called carnassials. As the jaws close, they slice meat into bite-sized chunks.

With its ears pricked slightly forwards, this wolf is listening for its next meal.

Wolves have long snouts, narrow chests and lean, slim bodies. Their whole shape is slender and smooth, which makes them fast runners. The thick fur all over their bodies keeps them warm and dry even when the weather is cold and wet.

Sense of smell

A wolf's sense of smell is much more powerful than a person's. It can identify thousands of different smells. Even young cubs can pick up the faint scent of distant animals. A wolf's keen hearing also helps it hunt its prey.

The paw prints, or pug marks, of a wolf's hind feet. The prints are in dried mud.

Wolves' relatives

Wolves and other wild dogs are all members of a larger group of animals called carnivorans. Cats, bears, raccoons and hyenas are also carnivorans.

⊕ The black-backed jackal lives in Africa. It can survive in very dry places, including deserts.

All these animals feed mainly on meat. About 40 to 50 million years ago a family of animals called the Miacoidea lived on Earth. They were about the same size and shape as modern mongooses and lived in trees. Scientists believe that gradually, over millions of years, they evolved (slowly changed) into swift-running hunters. These were the forerunners of modern dogs and wolves.

Jackals and foxes

There are more than 30 species (kinds) in the dog family. They include jackals, dingoes and foxes, which are all closely related to wolves. Wild dogs are found on every continent except Antarctica. Dingoes, the wild dogs that live in Australia, arrived there with humans more than 4,000 years ago.

All members of the dog family have good senses of smell and hearing. They feed mainly on meat and hunt live prey that they grip firmly with their sharp canine teeth. Most dogs have long legs, and all are strong runners. All have long snouts and furry coats, and most have long, bushy tails.

⊙ **The red fox is a smaller relative of the grey wolf. It often lives in city suburbs, where it feeds on rubbish as well as small animals.**

Dire wolves

Dire wolves lived in North America about two million years ago. They are now extinct, but we know that they existed from remains found in ancient tar pits in California. Dire wolves were giant predators, half as big again as modern wolves. They hunted prey as large as woolly mammoths.

Places where wolves live

Wolves live only in the northern hemisphere, the northern half of our planet. They were once much more common than they are now.

Wolves were once the world's most widespread predator. However, people have hunted them for thousands of years, so today they are much rarer. Wolves still live and hunt in parts of northern Europe, Asia and North America. Through the centuries wolves have been driven out of many areas as the land was taken over and used by people. In many places open

grasslands were ploughed to make fields for crops or fenced off to keep sheep and cattle. Elsewhere, forests were cut down for wood or to make space for towns and pastures. As more land was taken, wolves retreated to remote parts of the far north.

Wolf habitats

Across the northern hemisphere wolves live in many different types of country, from frozen wastes to snowy mountains, dark pine forests, leafy woodlands, rolling grasslands and even deserts.

🐾 **A pack of wolves attacks a muskox herd in a Canadian wilderness where few people live.**

Declining wolves

Wolves are still fairly common in Siberia, northern Russia, parts of Central Asia and, across the Atlantic Ocean, in Alaska and northern Canada where there are few people (the red areas of the map, above). Wolves once roamed across most of North America, Europe and Asia. They were once common in India, but only a few now live there.

Wolves of different colours

Grey wolves look slightly different according to where they live. For example, Arctic wolves are white in winter, while timber wolves remain grey.

Wolves from different areas also vary in size. Some are large, and others much smaller. The thickness of their fur varies too. Wolves that live in very cold places have thicker fur than wolves that live in warmer regions. These differences help the wolves survive in the areas where they live. Scientists think the size of different types of wolves is related to the size of the animals they hunt. Arctic wolves are the largest. They hunt muskoxen and caribou – some of the biggest prey.

Lots of colours

The colour of wolves' fur also varies from region to region. Some wolves have white or very pale fur. Others

Timber wolves live in the thick forests of North America. This wolf has darker grey fur than most wolves have.

A pack of Arctic wolves in their white winter coats.

are tawny, grey or black. Different types of wolves are often coloured so they blend with their surroundings. This camouflage (natural disguise) makes it easier for them to sneak up on their prey.

Wolves that live in deserts are often small and sand-coloured. Their pale coats reflect the Sun's rays, helping them keep cool and disguising them. Wolves that live in forests are medium-sized and often grey. The timber wolf of North America is an example.

Arctic wolves

Arctic or tundra wolves live in the snowy wastes of the far north. Their very thick coats help them keep warm in howling winds and freezing weather. All wolves shed their fur at certain times of year. They have a thick winter coat and a thin summer one. Arctic wolves' coats also change colour with the seasons. In summer many have dark fur. In winter they are pure white, so they can hide against the snow.

People and wolves

In early times, Native Americans admired wolves for their strength and cleverness. Many warriors and chiefs were named after wolves.

In medieval Europe things were very different. Before guns were invented, wolves were bolder and less scared of people. They would slink into lonely settlements to steal sheep, goats and cattle. Many people wrongly believed they also preyed on humans, particularly children.

Towns and villages hired special huntsmen to track and kill wolves with the help of large dogs. Later, the invention of guns made hunting easier. When European settlers arrived in North America, the same thing happened. Tens of thousands of wolves were shot, trapped or poisoned. Wolves were also killed for 'sport' – and for their warm fur.

Nothing to fear

In the last 50 years, there has been a change of attitude towards wolves. People realise we no longer need to fear them.

⚲ **A trainer with a wolf-dog. Wolf-dogs are a cross between a domestic dog and a wolf.**

⬆ **Many wolves are killed by vehicles when they try to cross roads. This dead timber wolf is being examined in Canada.**

⬅ **Wolf skins for sale in a Norwegian market.**

Domestic dogs

From toy poodles to giant St. Bernards, all breeds of domestic dogs are thought to be descended from the wolf. 'Man's best friend' has been around for at least 12,000 years. By Roman times, many breeds of dog had already appeared. Wolves and their close relatives, coyotes, dogs and dingoes, can all still interbreed to produce hybrids such as wolf-dogs.

Glossary

alpha female and male The most senior pair of animals in a wolf pack. The alpha pair are usually the only wolves to breed.

camouflage The colours and patterns on animals' bodies that blend with their surroundings and so help them hide from other animals.

canines The sharp, pointed teeth at the front sides of the wolf's mouth. The animal uses these to bite its prey.

carnivoran A large group of meat-eating animals that includes cats, dogs, bears, weasels and lions.

cub The young of animals such as wolves.

den A burrow used by animals such as wolves to protect their young.

evolve When an animal species changes over many generations so that the animals are better suited to the conditions in which they live.

habitat A type of area where certain animals live, such as a forest or a desert.

hierarchy A pecking order, or social order, among a group of animals.

litter A group of animals with the same mother, born at one time.

pack The name given to a group of wolves.

predator An animal that hunts other animals for food.

prey An animal that is hunted by other animals for food.

regurgitate When an animal vomits partly digested food to feed its young.

territory An area that an animal uses for feeding or for rearing its young. It defends this area against others of its kind. Many different animals use territories.

Further Reading

Books

A Pack of Wolves, and Other Canine Groups. Anna Claybourne. Basingstoke: Raintree, 2013.

Face to Face with Wolves. Jim and Judy Brandenburg. Washington D.C.: National Geographic, 2010.

My Best Book of Wolves and Wild Dogs. Christiane Gunzi. London: Kingfisher, 2003.

The Hidden Life of Wolves. James Dutcher. Washington D.C.: National Geographic, 2013.

Wolves. Emily Gravett. London: Macmillan, 2005.

Walk With a Wolf. Janni Howker. London: Walker, 2008.

Wolves. James Maclaine and John Francis. London: Usborne, 2013.

Websites

BBC Nature
Grey wolf videos, news and facts.
www.bbc.co.uk/nature/life/Gray_Wolf

International Wolf Centre
Wolf facts, news and photographs.
www.wolf.org

Wolf Education and Research Centre
A website concerned with wolf conservation.
www.wolfcenter.org

Wolf Park
A good summary of wolf lifestyle and anatomy. Some pages look more closely at wolves' relatives, including coyotes and foxes.
www.wolfpark.org

WorldWide Fund for Nature
Key facts about wolves, and ideas for protecting them in the wild.
wwf.panda.org/about_our_earth/species/profiles/mammals/wolf_timber_intro

Index